Affiliate marketing for beginners
2024

Guide for making money online

By

Darryl Rojas

TABLE OF CONTENTS

CHAPTER ONE 7
INTRODUCTION 7
    The definition of Affiliate Marketing 22
    The background of Affiliate Marketing 24
    Advantages-of-Affiliate Marketing 27
    Important Figures in Affiliate Marketing 32
CHAPTER TWO 36
    Choosing your Niche (Selecting your Specialization 36
    RESEARCHING AFFILIATE PROGRAMS 46
    Understanding-Affiliate Networks 47
    Signing-Up-for-Affiliate Programs 49
    CHAPTER THREE 52
Building Your Affiliate Marketing Platform 52
    Creating Compelling Content 52
    Building an Email List 53
    Establishing a Strong Social Media Presence 53
    Integrating YouTube Channels (if applicable): 54
CHAPTER FOUR 56
Creating High-Quality Content 56
    Writing Product Reviews 56
    Producing Information Guides and Tutorials ... 57
    Crafting-Compelling Calls-to-Action 58
    Incorporating Affiliate Links Strategically 59
CHAPTER FIVE 62
    Optimizing-for-Search Engines 62

Conducting Keyword Research.......................63
On-Page SEO Optimization............................ 64
Off-Page SEO Strategies................................ 65
Tracking and Analyzing SEO Performance.....66

CHAPTER SIX..68
Promoting Affiliate Links.................................. 68

1. Contextual Integration: Integrate affiliate links naturally within relevant content, such as blog posts, product reviews, and tutorials, to provide value to your audience and increase click-through rates..68

Utilizing Social Media Marketing...................... 69
Implementing Email Marketing Campaigns.....71
Leveraging Content Marketing Strategies.......72
Exploring Paid Advertising Options.................73

CHAPTER SEVEN.. 76
Best Practices and Strategies.......................... 76

1. Disclosing Affiliate Relationships................. 76
2. Focusing on Quality Content:......................77
3. Testing and Tracking Performance............. 79
4. Staying Updated with Industry Trends........ 80

CHAPTER EIGHT..82
Overcoming Challenges in Affiliate Marketing 82

Dealing with Competition................................ 83
Handling Rejection and Setbacks................... 84
Addressing-Regulatory,and Compliance Issues. 84

CHAPTER NINE.. 86

Advanced Affiliate Marketing Techniques....... 86
Exploring-Conversion-Rate Optimization (CRO).

3

88
Scaling Your Affiliate Marketing Business....... 89
Exploring Alternative Revenue Streams......... 89

CHAPTER TEN... 92
Affiliate Marketing Tools and Resources......... 92
1. Affiliate Networks and Platforms................. 92
2. SEO Tools and Analytic Software............... 93
3. Content Creation and Marketing Tools........94
4. Education Resources and Communities..... 96

CHAPTER ELEVEN... 98
Case Studies and Success Stories in Affiliate Marketing... 98
- Real-Life Examples of Successful Affiliate Marketers.. 98
- Strategies Behind Their Success.................98
- Lessons Learned and Key Takeaways......... 98

CHAPTER TWELVE... 104
Future Trends in Affiliate Marketing................104
1. Emerging Technology and Platforms........ 104
2. Prediction for the Future of Affiliate Marketing 106
3. Opportunities and Challenges Ahead....... 107

CHAPTER THIRTEEN.. 110
CONCLUSION... 110
Recap on the key content.............................110
Discussion Questions....................................114

Affiliate marketing presents an enticing opportunity for beginners to make money online by promoting products or services and earning commissions for successful referrals. This comprehensive guide will walk you through the basics of affiliate marketing and provide actionable tips to kickstart your journey to online success.

The above table of contents covers the topics and subtopics relevant to understanding, starting, and succeeding in affiliate marketing, providing a comprehensive guide for beginners and intermediate marketers alike.

Copyright © 2024 [Darryl Rojas].

All rights reserved. This content may not be reproduced, distributed, transmitted, displayed, or otherwise used without the prior written permission of the copyright owner.

CHAPTER ONE

INTRODUCTION

The Affiliate Journey

ABOUT DARRYL ROJAS BLOG

About Darryl Rojas & His Affiliate Marketing Success Story. Affiliate Marketing Success Story Hey everyone, it's Darryl here. Welcome to my site, where I get to brag about how awesome I am and talk about how great I am! But in all honesty, I've never felt completely comfortable talking or writing about myself; it just feels weird and sometimes like I'm being narcissistic. When I talk about how successful I've been in affiliate marketing, I also get unpleasant flashbacks of the past. You see, I have an embarrassing confession to make.

I used to fall for the same old get-rich-quick scams. You are aware of the individuals I refer to. The "gurus" who hold six-figure checks while standing in front of their Lamborghinis and promise to share their "secret" or "system," which anybody can, of course, accomplish with very little work? Yes, those individuals. Regretfully, I was duped into more than a few of those.

You now know that. Please don't condemn me!

long, slow breaths

I was sucked in even though I was a full-time, successful affiliate marketer previously. Even though the majority of them are selling snake oil—send me $4, and I'll teach you how to make money—that doesn't make them poor marketers. They're all excellent marketers, many of them. They display to you their beautiful automobiles, their actual six-figure checks, their outings with celebrities, etc.

That guy is not me, and I have no desire to act like him. Yes, affiliate marketing has helped me a lot, but I'm just an ordinary person. To be honest, I'm fine without an exotic car. My trusty old Chevy works perfectly for me.

In the end, I did build this website for financial gain, but I won't be selling you anything on this page. This is merely my sincere account of accomplishment with affiliate marketing. Nothing flashy, nothing hidden, nothing nonsense. I'm not sharing my affiliate marketing success story with you to try and sell you anything; rather, I'm just trying to demonstrate that anyone can actually make money online with affiliate marketing.

Despite the fact that sharing my story sometimes makes me uneasy, I frequently hear from people who say that they enjoyed it and found it inspiring. Now, let's get started.

As a Child, I Was A Little Sluggish
Indeed, I wasn't a bright child. Actually, I wasn't. I was born a few weeks late, and I learnt to walk, talk, and even crawl slowly! By the time I arrived at Kindergarten, everyone had a sneaking suspicion that something wasn't quite right about me.

I had to retake first grade since I lagged behind my peers so much. It destroyed any self-confidence a seven-year-old child could have, and it was awful for me. I can still clearly recall going to school the following year. I was asked why I was still in first grade by all of my former classmates, who were now in second grade. I also recall hearing children discussing me overheard. It was truly terrible.

That was only the beginning of my academic difficulties. My poor self-esteem made it difficult for me to have good social skills. I had a very terrible and lonely period in school.

It's astonishing that I made it through high school and barely graduated from college! Here is a copy of my official college transcript. I love that gorgeous 2.5 GPA!

My Recordings

Why, therefore, am I disclosing these private details about myself? since I am a person. I have benefits and drawbacks just like everybody else. I'm not "special" in any way. It's highly unlikely that I'm more intelligent than you. The main thing I have going for me is that I can write fairly well, but I was always in the half of the class that made the top half conceivable by most academic standards (thank you!).

A Boy Discovers the World!
Though it was difficult, I succeeded! After all those years of education, I not only graduated from high school but also somehow earned a college degree! Whoooo!

At this point, I took the reasonable course of action. After landing a high-profile office job, I quickly reversed my student loan debt by taking out a zero-down payment loan on a $30,000 sports automobile.

It found out that my posh office job was really just a glorified telemarketer job. After two dreadful years, I got laid off in the middle of the worst recession since the Great Depression, with over $50,000 in debt from my new car and college loans on top of some extra credit card debt I had accrued. Enjoyable.

Finally, I rapidly came to the conclusion that working in an office building would slowly kill me through mental torment. I had just graduated from college, broke, and sad. I owed tens of thousands of dollars, and I had no idea what I wanted to do with my life. I didn't have much fun during this.

I was finally able to pursue my passion and excel at truck driving.

I gave it a lot of thought before deciding to take a bold action. I made the decision to become an over-the-road truck driver when I was completely broke. Yeah, so much for that nice degree from college!

I ended up paying for my truck driving school with my unemployment benefits. Regretfully, my employer successfully contested my job benefits and prevailed. I was told to repay the $2,000 in benefits that they had already disbursed. Higher debt. Enjoyable!

I gave it a lot of thought before deciding to take a bold action. I made the decision to become an over-the-road truck driver when I was completely broke. Yeah, so much for that nice degree from college!

I ended up paying for my truck driving school with my unemployment benefits. Regretfully, my employer successfully contested my job benefits and prevailed. I was told to repay the $2,000 in benefits that they had already disbursed. Higher debt. Enjoyable!

Despite its absurdity, this choice was the best one I have ever made for myself. Driving a truck is a serious job. Although it's a challenging work, I truly enjoyed it. I've always wanted to know what it would be like to go across the stunning nations of Canada and the United States in a large truck. I practically lived out of my truck and traveled constantly for the following two years. It was incredible, and I went everywhere. This is a photo of my vehicle. I still really do miss it sometimes.

My Vehicle

The Beginning Of My Own Network Marketing Company
I started writing a blog for TruckingTruth when I first started driving trucks. I did this because I wanted to support those who were thinking about becoming truck drivers, not because I was looking for money.

Following some time spent posting on TruckingTruth, recording my truck driving experiences, and picking up the basics, I figured, what the heck, why not make my own website and see how it goes!

I wrote content for my own website every spare moment I had for the next six months. I was writing whether I had to wait for a fresh load assignment. I was writing if my truck was being loaded or unloaded with cargo. I wrote a few articles after putting in a full 11 hours of driving.

In order to record my trucking career, I also made a YouTube account.

And then at last it did. I once received a $7 royalty. I was really taken aback! Although it took me six months to earn the initial $7, it demonstrated to me that earning money online is indeed feasible. All I had to do was press on, and that's exactly what I did!

Giving Up My Career As A Truck Driver To Focus On Affiliate Marketing Full-Time
I was making roughly $2k a month online in just 11 months after I launched my website and 3 months after receiving my first commission.

By now, things were really starting to pile up. I made the decision to try life one more time. In order to complement my affiliate marketing income until I could increase it even more, I quit my full-time work as a truck driver and took up a part-time freelance job.

I then started to grow by creating even more websites. I started by using the money I made from my first website to buy SharkSider.com. Then, in addition to a few other smaller "micro-niche" websites, I founded DogFoodInsider.com, CatFoodInsider.com, DogHealthInsider.com, and DogObedienceInsider.com.

I eventually stopped working as a freelancer on the side after roughly 14 months so that I could devote all of my attention to my own business. By this time, I was almost debt free as well. Thanks in large part to affiliate marketing, a dream realized!

Returning to the Road!
The independence that affiliate marketing offers is a major factor in my desire to be successful at it. I used to be envious of the RVs traveling down the road when I was just starting my business and still driving a truck. That's my desire. Total freedom. I would be able to travel in true luxury and go wherever I want, whenever I want, and stay for whatever

long I want. That was my ultimate objective, and I could finally achieve it.

I went on a road trip in style after buying a brand-new travel trailer and a well-used truck in excellent condition!

My Hitch And Truck

This is how the interior appeared. If I may say so myself, this mobile office isn't too bad!

Within the Trailer

I spent a few years traveling the length and breadth of the United States with my dog, and I had an absolute joy. I inhabited deserts, mountains, woods, and pretty much any other place I felt like it. I could work from almost anywhere at all. Not only that, but as I led this amazing lifestyle, my income kept rising. These are a few of the locations I visited.

Locations I've Visited

I shot the video below a few years ago from one of my favorite locations on earth. The little-known treasure of a location in the Colorado Rocky Mountains is Vallecito.

For me, the lifestyle affiliate marketing has been nothing less than a dream. Undoubtedly, achieving success in affiliate marketing has required a great deal of work, but it has also given me unparalleled flexibility. There are just no other jobs that I am aware of that offer this kind of freedom and compensation.

Profits From Affiliate Marketing During 7 Years

Many individuals are curious about long-term success stories from affiliate marketers. While everyone has a different definition of what "long-term" really means, I received my first $7 commission in June 2011 and my company has not only survived the years but has also seen nearly annual profits growth.

I'm also more diverse than I've ever been. I collaborate with over a dozen affiliate partners on roughly a dozen distinct websites. This is a much better option than managing a firm that solely makes money from one product or service or working for one that might fire me at any time.

I Never Would Have Imagined Becoming A Super Story in Affiliate Marketing

If you want affiliate marketing badly enough, you too could become a success story. I never imagined myself to be a success in affiliate marketing. My only goal was to make enough money to live off of without having to work for someone else. Heck, I would have even accepted a respectable part-time wage that I could augment with a low-key part-time gig.

I am aware that this adage is frequently overdone, but if I can accomplish this, so can you.

My Best Suggestion To Become A Super Story In Affiliate Marketing

Be patient! That is my top recommendation for anyone hoping to achieve success with affiliate marketing on their own. You must exercise patience. This enterprise functions similarly to all other enterprises. What, a few years are the average turnaround time for tiny enterprises to start making a profit? It is true that affiliate marketing is a viable business that can bring in six or even seven figures, but you shouldn't expect to achieve that without months or even years of diligent labor and perseverance.

For whatever reason, most affiliate marketers never succeed because they give up. The majority of people have a lot of motivation for the first few weeks, but after that, life interferes, other priorities take precedence, and affiliate marketing enterprises fail miserably.

Do You Want To Know More?
I promised not to try to sell you anything on this page at the beginning of the post, and I'm keeping my word. I just wanted to encourage you and demonstrate that it is absolutely feasible to make money with affiliate marketing by sharing my affiliate marketing success story with you. I hope I was able to demonstrate that I'm not some unique individual or that I know more than you. I'm just an ordinary guy who happened to believe anything will work after giving it some time. Was I simply fortunate? Perhaps so, but I've been able to repeatedly accomplish this.

Now that I've made good on my promise not to sell you anything, enjoy my free guide on how to launch an affiliate marketing blog. Not quite ready to launch your website or blog? For your consideration, here are some more resources:

7 Reputable Online Income Generation Strategies - Want to earn money online but lack the time to establish an affiliate marketing business? It may surprise you to learn that there are many real, authentic ways to generate money online—I'm not talking about pointless surveys or multi-level marketing nonsense.

These are seven genuine ways to start earning money online right away.

Causes of Affiliate Marketers' Failure Regretfully, there are unethical affiliate marketers. These are a few of the bad reasons for affiliate marketing. Don't be one of the awful affiliate marketers who make the rest of us seem bad if you decide to pursue this career.

How To Find Profitable Affiliate Marketing Niche - Your earning potential from affiliate marketing is primarily determined by the specialized market you choose to target. This post offers some advice on how to identify a profitable niche market to increase your chances of making a solid online income.

Is the Work Put Into Affiliate Marketing Worth It? Marketing with affiliates is not quick or simple. Running an affiliate marketing business requires time and attention to detail, much like any other business. Given how difficult it is to run a business, is affiliate marketing really worth the effort? Find out how much work it actually requires and make your own decision.

How Much Time Does It Actually Take To Make Money Online? Numerous experts claim to be able to teach you how to quickly make money online. I am not among them. This is my "no B.S." response regarding the true time it takes to generate income online.

That's my tale of success with affiliate marketing, and I'm sticking with it!
I hope my affiliate marketing success story was inspiring, or at the absolute least, thought-provoking. Why are you still reading this if not?

There's no reason you can't be successful in affiliate marketing too, if you enter the field with the appropriate expectations and resources. Your perspective on money and your life will be completely transformed once you begin earning money while you sleep, I assure you. Your efforts have truly paid off.

The definition of Affiliate Marketing

We discuss what is meant by affiliate marketing. The process of Affiliate Marketing. and how to do it properly, whether you're a novice or an expert.

Then, what does the term affiliate marketing mean?

Affiliate marketing is the practice of making money by endorsing a third-party product or service in exchange for a commission. In a sense, you are the product's marketer. The amount the business pays you is determined on the sales generated by your advertising. This is an excellent method of earning some terrific passive money from goods, apps, and platforms that you genuinely believe in and use on a regular basis. Additionally, discuss them briefly at first; don't thrust yourself into making the pitch.

You have to trust someone if you follow them and they recommend a product to you four or five times before trying to sell it to you.

Conversely, it doesn't appear very genuine if they suddenly say, "BUY THIS!"

But I have witnessed far too many mistakes being made. Don't be one of those persons who advertises something just because the profit margin is large. Only advocate for what you genuinely appreciate and believe in. Additionally, confirm that it makes sense for your audience and is pertinent to your blog or business.

By simply posting links in Facebook groups, you may use your social media accounts to promote affiliate products (of course, in a relevant manner; first, make sure to read the community rules!). Alternatively, you might do it through pertinent blog entries on your website. If the only source of income for their firm is commissions from sales, some even go so far as to design entire marketing campaigns for affiliate products. Affiliate links and blog content can be effectively promoted using Pinterest pins. But do watch out that you don't come out to your audience as "spammy." Nobody is fooled by a spamming affiliate

The background of Affiliate Marketing

Because it is such an inconspicuous way to make money, affiliate marketing has a strong claim to be the most lucrative revenue stream you've never heard of. Typically, a publisher adds a piece of code to the footer of their website and automatically starts to be rewarded when one of their articles is responsible for a purchase on a brand's website that it links to. You might see a disclaimer here or a line item in revenue reports from a profitable digital native publisher there, but otherwise it gets overlooked.

Although the name seems very technical, it has been there for a while and is, in our opinion, a cash stream that publishers shouldn't pass up. Check out the background of this most modest of income sources instead of taking our word for it.

The year 1989 marks several significant events in our story, including the fall of the Berlin Wall,

Madonna's rendition of "Like a Prayer," and William J. Tobin.

The year in question saw the founding of PC Flowers & Gifts, a little-known business that is now remembered. He is known as the "Father of Modern Affiliate Marketing." It was the first company in history to have an affiliate program and sold flowers online. It was the seventh venture that he had created out of 10 since 1968. It generated over $6 million in sales by 1991, and by 1998, it had about 3000 affiliate marketing partners.

Like any other e-commerce invention, Amazon followed suit quickly. It introduced Amazon Associates in 1996, which went on to become a model for other firms starting their own affiliate programs. To this day, it is one of the major players in the affiliate industry.

In 1998, bigger affiliate networks like Commission Junction emerged. Initially, these companies made it possible for publishers to make money through affiliate relationships and for advertisers to manage their affiliate programs.

Since then, affiliate marketing's history has developed in tandem with the expansion of the internet. The advent of e-commerce in the late

1990s, the increase of online publication in the 2000s, the development of cookies, and the emergence of influencers in 2010 have all contributed to the $12 billion industry that is affiliate marketing.

From its humble beginnings as a social shopping tool, Skimlinks quickly evolved into a platform that allowed publishers to use affiliate marketing to generate substantial commerce revenues from product-related content they wrote. Since its launch in 2007, Skimlinks has grown into a legitimate commerce platform with a range of solutions to help publishers earn even more from affiliate marketing; in fact, we no longer even mention affiliate marketing on a daily basis—instead, we talk about "commerce content" and our tools that help publishers help their readers while also making more money.

In addition to helping publishers monetize Google AMP pages, we now provide a price comparison tool and an editorial service wherein our Chief Editor assists publishers in producing commerce content.

The top publishers in the industry have advanced to the point where, in recent years, they have separated out commerce content into a separate, specialized brand. Because of their enormous popularity, publishers such as New York Magazine can commit entire editorial teams and brands to producing commerce content, which generates up to 25 percent of their revenue via affiliate marketing.

This brings the present day to our attention. In a short period of time, affiliate marketing has advanced significantly and outlasted other, more well-known revenue streams (hey, display advertising!). Furthermore, it is still rising. This trip suggestions guide book is perfect for you as a beginner if you'd want to learn more about affiliate marketing and how you may use it for your own website.

Advantages-of-Affiliate Marketing

If you've worked in the e-commerce industry for any length of time, you've probably heard of affiliate marketing, but many people aren't quite sure what it is or how the process operates. To put it simply, affiliate marketing is a performance-based marketing model that pays affiliate partners for encouraging desired actions, such as site visits, lead form completion, and/or converted sales. Affiliate marketing can be a very profitable and low-risk way to advertise your products.

We've put together a list of the top 5 advantages of affiliate marketing to assist you realize its true benefits:

1. **Affiliate marketing is dependent on performance**
An affiliate program's primary benefit is that it is totally performance-based. Affiliates are more inclined to drive the target conversion because they only get paid a commission once the desired activity is completed. This guarantees that you get what you paid for and mitigates any efforts that generate traffic that has little to no value for your business.

2. It facilitates audience expansion

In every industry and product category that exists today, there are affiliates. There are always appropriate websites to align with, whether your goal is to enter into the retail market or something more specialized like handcrafted vintage toys. Many of these affiliates will already have a loyal following of visitors, which is fantastic news. These collaborations provide you the chance to further penetrate your current target markets or branch out into new ones that you might not have had the time to investigate, strengthening your brand's online presence. Consider these collaborators as an addition to your present sales or marketing staff.

3. Affiliates can improve your standing

You can enhance the reputation of your company and its merchandise by collaborating with reliable bloggers and respectable websites. These collaborators will support your offerings and, in our opinion, help to increase customer trust in your good or service. Customers are more inclined to believe the advice of a third party during the research stage of a purchase than content created by the website offering the product. Additionally, customers have some faith in the websites that they frequently visit to get product recommendations.

4. **It is reasonably priced.**
For the reasons mentioned above, affiliate marketing has the potential to be incredibly economical. You're not wasting ad money on places that have no track record of success if you're only paying commissions when the intended conversion happens. Additionally, finding affiliates in new markets is a simple approach to enter that market without having to incur the overhead costs of launching a full marketing campaign,

which reduces the need to invest funds in an untested market for testing.

5. Affiliates can quickly scale your traffic (and sales) Recruiting affiliates to your program will help you scale traffic faster in conjunction with your other marketing efforts. The more sites that link to your pages, the more opportunities you'll have to convert those users into paid customers. Additionally, although affiliate links won't directly affect your search engine rankings, they will have a "halo effect," meaning that more people will find your products and visit your pages, which is great for your rankings. You can almost always expect a boost to your direct and organic traffic as well as a higher level of referral traffic.

Important Figures in Affiliate Marketing

1. **Affiliates**:
Also referred to as publishers, affiliates are people or organizations that advertise the goods or services of other businesses in exchange for commissions from purchases or recommendations.

2. **Merchants**:
Sometimes referred to as advertisers or merchants, merchants are businesses that sell goods or services and provide affiliate programs as a means of encouraging others to spread the word about them. Increased visibility, traffic, and sales brought about by affiliates' marketing initiatives are advantageous to merchants.

3. **Affiliate Networks**:

Affiliate networks are intermediaries that connect affiliates with merchants and manage affiliate programs on behalf of merchants. Affiliate networks provide tracking, reporting, and payment solutions, as well as access to a network of affiliates and merchants.

4. **Clients**:

Clients are the final consumers who buy goods or services via affiliate links that affiliates give. Consumers gain from affiliates' suggestions and evaluations since they are able to make well-informed purchases.

5. **Tracking and Technology Providers**:

Tracking and technology providers develop and maintain tracking technology, such as cookies, tracking pixels, and affiliate tracking software, that enable merchants to accurately track and attribute sales to specific affiliates.

6. **Regulatory and Compliance Entities**:
Regulatory and compliance entities, such as the Federal Trade Commission (FTC) in the United States, enforce regulations and guidelines related to affiliate marketing, including disclosure requirements and consumer protection laws.

CHAPTER TWO

Getting Started with Affiliate Marketing

Starting an affiliate marketing business is an exciting venture that can lead to flexibility and financial freedom. But getting started needs thorough preparation, investigation, and calculated choices. We'll go over all the necessary procedures to get started with affiliate marketing in this in-depth guide, including selecting your specialty, looking into affiliate programs, comprehending affiliate networks, and registering for affiliate programs.

Choosing your Niche (Selecting your Specialization

A crucial first step in your affiliate marketing journey is selecting the appropriate niche. Your chosen niche will define your target market, the products you recommend, and, eventually, the level of success you have in the affiliate marketing industry.

After giving you a brief overview of affiliate marketing, I'll guide you in selecting the ideal affiliate niche.

1. Take Your Interests and Knowledge Into Account

The first thing I usually advise is looking at your areas of competence and interest. Why do people visit your blog and what is the content of your site? Which areas of your knowledge do your readers trust the most?

For example, you would probably not get very far attempting to promote rock climbing equipment if you were a culinary writer. However, you stand a strong chance of earning money from merchants selling premium cooking pots and utensils.

Food preparation affiliate programs

Your blog would be ideal as an affiliate niche if it included the kinds of products you enjoy and use on a regular basis in your kitchen. Because you have established yourself as an authority in your subject, your readers will trust your recommendation and you will be able to market a product you genuinely believe in.

2. **Assess Monetization and Profitability**
Assessing the profitability of your intended affiliate niche is the next stage.

Will Consumers Purchase the Items in Your Affiliate Market?
You would need to determine whether the things you wish to promote will result in sales, using the food blogger as an example from before.

The likelihood of the response being yes is high. Since everyone eats, being a food blogger has certain advantages. Although most people don't purchase pricey kitchenware, most do cook at least a couple nights a week. You will probably turn a profit even if you promote both pricey and cheap kitchen products if they result in a large volume of sales.

However, you won't generate much money in that affiliate area if all you offer are niche kitchen products that very few people use or desire.

Here are a few more methods to determine whether a product has a market:

1. Is the product good? The first and most important thing to consider when selecting lucrative

affiliate programs is whether the product is worthwhile advertising. It won't sell well if it malfunctions frequently or breaks readily. Promoting a subpar product also puts you at danger of losing future revenue.

2. Is it being promoted by your rivals? There's a good chance that a product or service has a market if other people are recommending it.

3. Is the product selling well? You may not have access to this information for every affiliate, but many sellers will share how well their products are selling. Skimlinks has created a Trending products report that you can filter by "Most popular" to see which products are currently selling the most across their entire network.

4. Test products: One of the best ways to determine whether there is a market in your niche is to pitch products to your audience. Promote goods you firmly believe in, then watch how your audience reacts. Does it convert to sales, or do people mostly ignore the posts you share about them?

Further more;
Does the Affiliate Pay Well? Another thing to think about is how much the affiliate program pays. Some programs pay very little per sale, meaning

you would need to convert a tonne of readers to make a profit. Even with a high traffic website, an affiliate program that pays poorly will not result in high profits and will ultimately be a frustrating experience. One way to help prevent working with low-paying affiliates is to use Earnings Per Click (EPC), which is provided by Skimlinks for every merchant so publishers can rapidly determine if they're worth their time.

1. **Examine the Rivals** (Yourselves and Other Affiliate Programs)
It's time to research the competitors once you've identified a few goods or services you want to promote. This entails researching the rival programs for both your affiliate program and yourself.

2. **Examine the Competition for the Affiliate Program**
I've decided to utilize Bluehost and Dreamhost as my two main hosting providers on my blog because I trust and use them.

It was necessary for me to conduct research to determine whether Bluehost and Dreamhost were worthwhile affiliate programs to use. Are they hosting plans well-liked enough to compete with other hosting plans, and were they programs that my readers would find appealing?

3. Research Your Competition

If you know the product you want to promote does well against its competition, the next step is to research what kind of competition you will have in this affiliate niche. How many bloggers are currently endorsing the good or service that you wish to collaborate on? Bluehost and Dreamhost have demonstrated that they are quality products with great reviews. People consistently prefer these companies and are happy with their performance. This convinced me that it would be a worthwhile product to advertise on my website and that it would facilitate conversions.

Many people in my situation are advertising hosting options. In order to compete with the numerous other sites that were endorsing hosting affiliate schemes, I had to assess whether my blog was getting enough interest and traffic. If not, I had to determine what steps I needed to take to improve my blog's visibility.

Finding an affiliate topic with very less competition is something I would advise new bloggers to do in order to increase their chances of making sales. This is also known as "looking for market gaps," which I'll address in the section that follows.

4. **Examine Affiliate Niche Market Gaps**

A excellent starting point for choosing the ideal affiliate niche for your site is to consider the gaps in the market.

When something people need but aren't getting, there is a market gap. For instance, there was a void in the market for face masks at the start of the pandemic. Although there were many people who wanted to buy masks, not many companies were selling them in large quantities.

The gap in the market for blogging and affiliate marketing would be the absence of reviews for goods or services that consumers are genuinely interested in. In order to choose whether or not to trust a product, readers rely on bloggers to offer honest, thorough reviews. They want to determine whether the desired product is worth the money they plan to spend.

How are holes in the market found? Here are some pointers:

Follow the current fashions. There won't be as many reviews or affiliate partners for recent releases or popular items. Now is an excellent moment to produce advertising for these products.
Engage in conversation. Engage readers who are interested in the niche of your blog. What are their

desires? What, they claim, isn't being supplied at this time?

Take some time to look things up on Google. Which items would you like to advocate for? Visit Google to find out what kind of material has previously been published about such topics.

Look into social media. What topics are people discussing on Facebook, Twitter, Instagram, Reddit, Quora, and TikTok? People on social media will tell you what's going on if you want to know the inside scoop.

Consider the distinct issues you can resolve. Which issues are present in your specialty that you are aware of? In what innovative method might your possible affiliate partner address those issues?

5. **Select High Purchase Intent Keywords with Low to Medium Competition**

Google needs to be considered while promoting goods or services on your blog. That entails being mindful of SEO, or search engine optimization.

There are three things you should consider:

Are they looking for it?
Do consumers have a strong desire to purchase it?
Is there a lot of competition for this phrase (can you rank well in a Google search)?

You utilize keywords or keyword phrases to tell Google what kind of material you have. Throughout your writing, you'll frequently use the same keywords multiple times, particularly in titles and headlines.

You won't merely be writing a typical review of the good or service you're endorsing as an affiliate partner. While writing a typical review is a good idea, there are other ways to market it as well. For instance, I've mentioned hosting plans in several of my blog entries, such as these:

These are all popular keyword phrases that people search for on Google, so it makes sense for me to promote my affiliate partners using them. The keywords you choose should be something that people do search for, but it doesn't have to generate millions of searches a month to be worthwhile. What matters is that you have a good chance of ranking well for them and that they drive traffic to an affiliate product you can promote. 15 Best Hosting Plans for Bloggers. How Much Does Web Hosting Cost? What is WordPress? These are all popular keyword phrases that people search for on Google, so naturally, they give me the opportunity to promote my affiliate partners.

To increase my chances of increasing my affiliate marketing revenue, I've increased the number of affiliate programs I promote over time and keep looking for new content topics with low-to-medium competition and somewhat high purchase intent. Use Google Keyword Planner: This is a useful tool that can be used to look up keywords and keyword phrases. It can tell you how many people are searching for a particular keyword and whether it has low or high competition. It also has a section called "suggested bid," which gives you an idea of how much marketers might be willing to pay per click.

6. Never Undervalue the Power of Video

For bloggers today, YouTube videos are a natural fit. Videos are popular and a perfect addition to your blog or affiliate area.

Creating videos that discuss your experience with a tool, product, or service that you can recommend as an affiliate is a terrific way to do two things:
(1) expand your audience on platforms like YouTube; and
(2) provide your readers with an alternative form of engagement to textual material.

Together with my comprehensive tutorial on how to establish a blog, I've also made a detailed YouTube video that explains the concepts in visual form. In addition to engaging readers who prefer visual or video material, this helps me reach new audiences and improve my SEO because blog posts with videos typically rank somewhat higher on Google searches.

RESEARCHING AFFILIATE PROGRAMS

1. **Identify Relevant Merchants**: Start by identifying merchants or brands within your niche that offer affiliate programs. Look for reputable companies with quality products or services that align with your niche and audience.

2. **Explore Affiliate Networks**: Explore affiliate networks such as ShareASale, Commission Junction, ClickBank, and Amazon Associates, which serve as intermediaries connecting affiliates with merchants. Browse their directories to find affiliate programs within your niche.

3. **Assess Program Terms and Conditions**: Before joining an affiliate program, carefully review the program terms and conditions. Pay attention to commission rates, payment methods, cookie durations, promotional guidelines, and any restrictions or requirements imposed by the merchant.

4. **Check Merchant Reputation and Track Record**: Research the reputation and track record of merchants offering affiliate programs. Look for merchants with a positive reputation, reliable tracking systems, and a history of timely payments to affiliates.

5. **Read Reviews and Testimonials**: Seek out reviews and testimonials from other affiliates who have participated in the affiliate programs you're considering. Pay attention to feedback regarding program performance, support, and overall satisfaction.

Understanding-Affiliate Networks

Affiliate networks play a crucial role in the affiliate marketing ecosystem by facilitating connections between affiliates and merchants and providing essential tools and resources to manage affiliate programs effectively.

1. **Role of Affiliate Networks**: Affiliate networks serve as intermediaries between affiliates and merchants, providing a platform for merchants to

list their affiliate programs and for affiliates to discover and join those programs.

2. **Benefits of Affiliate Networks**: Affiliate networks offer several benefits for both affiliates and merchants. For affiliates, affiliate networks provide access to a wide range of affiliate programs, consolidated reporting and tracking, payment processing, and support services. For merchants, affiliate networks offer access to a network of affiliates, tracking and reporting tools, and streamlined management of affiliate programs.

3. **Types of Affiliate Networks**: There are different types of affiliate networks, including general affiliate networks that cater to a wide range of industries and verticals, as well as niche affiliate networks that specialize in specific niches or verticals.

4. **Popular Affiliate Networks**: Some of the most popular affiliate networks include ShareASale, Commission Junction (CJ Affiliate), Rakuten Advertising (formerly LinkShare), ClickBank, and Amazon Associates. Each network has its own unique features, strengths, and focus areas, so it's essential to research and compare networks to find the best fit for your needs.

5. **Joining Affiliate Networks**: To join an affiliate network, simply visit the network's website

and sign up for an affiliate account. You'll typically need to provide some basic information about yourself and your website or promotional channels. Once your account is approved, you can start browsing affiliate programs and applying to join those that align with your niche and interests.

Signing-Up-for-Affiliate Programs

After researching affiliate programs and understanding affiliate networks, the final step is to sign up for affiliate programs that align with your niche, audience, and promotional channels.

1. **Review Program Requirements**: Before applying to join an affiliate program, review the program requirements and eligibility criteria. Some programs may have specific requirements regarding website traffic, content quality, promotional methods, or geographic location.

2. **Complete the Application Process**: To apply for an affiliate program, visit the merchant's website or affiliate network platform and complete the application process. You may need to provide information about your website or promotional

channels, traffic metrics, and promotional strategies.

3. **Wait for Approval**: After submitting your application, wait for the merchant or affiliate network to review and approve your application. The approval process may take anywhere from a few days to a few weeks, depending on the program and the volume of applications.

4. **Access Affiliate Resources**: Once your application is approved, you'll gain access to affiliate resources such as tracking links, banners, promotional materials, and reporting tools. Familiarize yourself with these resources and start integrating affiliate links into your content or promotional channels.

5. **Start Promoting**: With your affiliate links in hand, you're ready to start promoting the merchant's products or services to your audience. Create compelling content, reviews, tutorials, or promotional campaigns that highlight the benefits of the products or services and encourage your audience to make a purchase through your affiliate links.

In conclusion, getting started with affiliate marketing involves choosing your niche, researching affiliate programs, understanding affiliate networks, and signing up for affiliate programs that align with your niche, audience, and promotional channels. By following these steps and investing time and effort into building relationships with merchants and promoting their products effectively, you can embark on a successful affiliate marketing journey and unlock the potential for passive income and financial freedom.

CHAPTER THREE

Building Your Affiliate Marketing Platform

Your affiliate marketing platform serves as the central hub for your online business endeavors. Begin by selecting a niche that aligns with your interests, expertise, and market demand. Conduct thorough research to identify profitable affiliate programs within your chosen niche.

Next, establish a professional blog or website to showcase your content and affiliate offerings. Choose a reliable web hosting service and a user-friendly content management system (CMS) such as WordPress. Invest time in crafting a visually appealing design and optimizing your site for search engines (SEO).

Creating Compelling Content

Content is the lifeblood of your affiliate marketing platform. Produce high-quality, valuable content that resonates with your target audience. This may include informative articles, product reviews, tutorials, comparison guides, and engaging multimedia content.

Focus on addressing the pain points and needs of your audience, offering actionable insights, and demonstrating genuine expertise. Incorporate relevant keywords strategically to improve organic visibility and attract qualified traffic to your site.

Building an Email List

An email list is a powerful asset for nurturing relationships with your audience and driving affiliate sales. Implement lead capture mechanisms such as opt-in forms, exit-intent pop-ups, and content upgrades to encourage visitors to subscribe to your mailing list.

Offer valuable incentives such as exclusive content, discounts, or free resources in exchange for email sign-ups. Segment your email list based on user preferences and behaviors to deliver targeted, personalized content and promotions.

Establishing a Strong Social Media Presence

Social media platforms offer invaluable opportunities for expanding your reach, building brand awareness, and engaging with your audience. Choose platforms that resonate with your target demographic and align with your content strategy.

Create compelling profiles that reflect your brand identity and values. Consistently share a mix of curated content, original creations, affiliate promotions, and interactive posts to keep your audience engaged. Leverage hashtags, influencer partnerships, and paid advertising to amplify your reach and drive traffic to your affiliate links.

Integrating YouTube Channels (if applicable):

YouTube presents a dynamic platform for creating engaging video content and connecting with a diverse audience. If video content aligns with your strategy and resources, consider launching a YouTube channel dedicated to your niche.

Produce high-quality videos that entertain, educate, or inspire your viewers. Incorporate affiliate links in your video descriptions and encourage viewers to explore further or make a purchase. Optimize your videos for search visibility by using relevant keywords, engaging thumbnails, and compelling titles.

Lastly,

Building a successful affiliate marketing platform requires strategic planning, consistent effort, and a deep understanding of your audience's needs and preferences. By creating compelling content, cultivating an engaged email list, establishing a strong social media presence, and potentially integrating YouTube channels, you can position yourself for long-term success in the competitive world of affiliate marketing. Stay committed to providing value and fostering genuine connections with your audience, and you'll unlock the full potential of your affiliate marketing empire.

CHAPTER FOUR

Creating High-Quality Content

Content is king in the world of affiliate marketing. The ability to create compelling, valuable content lies at the heart of driving traffic, engaging audiences, and ultimately, generating affiliate revenue. In this guide, we'll delve into the art of crafting high-quality content for affiliate marketing, covering the creation of product reviews, information guides, tutorials, crafting effective calls-to-action (CTAs), and strategically incorporating affiliate links.

Writing Product Reviews

Product reviews are a cornerstone of affiliate marketing content, offering audiences valuable insights into the benefits, features, and drawbacks of various products or services. To create impactful product reviews, follow these key steps:

1. **Research**: Thoroughly research the product or service you're reviewing, exploring its features, specifications, pricing, and user feedback.

2. **Personal Experience**: Whenever possible, incorporate your own experiences and opinions to provide authentic perspectives.

3. **Structure**: Organize your review with a clear structure, including an introduction, overview of the product, pros and cons, and a final recommendation.

4. **Visuals**: Supplement your review with high-quality images or multimedia elements to enhance engagement and visual appeal.

5. **Transparency**: Disclose your affiliate relationship with honesty and transparency to build trust with your audience.

Producing Information Guides and Tutorials

Information guides and tutorials serve as valuable resources that educate and empower your audience, positioning you as a trusted authority in your niche. Here's how to create effective guides and tutorials:

1. **Identify Topics**: Identify topics that address common pain points, questions, or interests within your niche.

2. **Comprehensive Content**: Provide comprehensive, in-depth information that addresses the needs of your audience. Divide complicated ideas into manageable steps.

3. **Visual Aids**: Use visuals, diagrams, screenshots, or video tutorials to supplement your written content and enhance comprehension.

4. **Actionable Advice**: Offer actionable tips, strategies, and solutions that your audience can implement immediately to achieve their goals.

5. **Engagement**: Encourage interaction and engagement by inviting questions, feedback, and comments from your audience.

Crafting-Compelling Calls-to-Action

Effective calls-to-action (CTAs) are essential for guiding your audience towards desired actions, whether it's making a purchase, subscribing to your email list, or sharing your content. Here are some tips for crafting compelling CTAs:

1. **Clarity**: Ensure your CTAs are clear, concise, and easy to understand. Use action verbs to prompt immediate action.

2. **Value Proposition**: Clearly communicate the benefits or incentives of taking the desired action.

3. **Urgency**: Create a sense of urgency or scarcity to motivate your audience to act quickly.

4. **Placement**: Strategically place your CTAs throughout your content, including within product reviews, guides, and tutorials.

5. **Testing and Optimization**: Continuously test different CTAs, messaging, and placement to optimize performance and maximize conversions.

Incorporating Affiliate Links Strategically

Strategic placement of affiliate links is crucial for monetizing your content effectively without compromising user experience or credibility. The following are some guidelines for adding affiliate links:

1. **Relevance**: Ensure that affiliate links are contextually relevant to the content and provide genuine value to your audience.

2. **Natural Integration**: Integrate affiliate links seamlessly within your content, avoiding intrusive or spammy placement.

3. **Disclosures**: Clearly disclose your affiliate relationships to maintain transparency and comply with legal regulations.

4. **Tracking**: Utilize tracking tools provided by affiliate networks to monitor link performance and optimize your strategy.

5. **Diversification**: Experiment with different types of affiliate links, including text links, banner ads, and product recommendations, to determine what resonates best with your audience.

CHAPTER FIVE

Mastering the SEO for affiliate marketing success

Optimizing-for-Search Engines

Search engine optimization (SEO) plays a pivotal role in the success of affiliate marketing endeavors. It involves a range of techniques aimed at improving a website's visibility in search engine results pages (SERPs). To optimize your affiliate marketing content for search engines, consider the following strategies:

1. **Content Quality**: Produce high-quality, relevant content that addresses the needs and interests of your target audience.

2. **Keywords**: Incorporate relevant keywords naturally throughout your content, including in titles, headings, meta tags, and body text.

3. **Mobile Optimization**: Ensure your website is mobile-friendly, as mobile usability is a key ranking factor for search engines.

4. **Site Speed**: Optimize page load times to improve user experience and search engine rankings.

5. **User Experience**: Provide a seamless, intuitive user experience by organizing content logically, optimizing navigation, and minimizing intrusive ads.

Conducting Keyword Research

Keyword research is the foundation of effective SEO strategy, helping you identify the terms and phrases your target audience is searching for. Follow these steps to conduct keyword research for affiliate marketing:

1. **Brainstorm**: Start by brainstorming potential keywords and topics related to your niche and affiliate products.

2. **Keyword Tools**: Use keyword research tools such as Google Keyword Planner, SEMrush, or Ahrefs to discover relevant keywords, analyze search volume, and assess competition.

3. **Long-Tail Keywords**: Target long-tail keywords, which are longer, more specific phrases that typically have lower competition and higher conversion potential.

4. **Competitive Analysis**: Analyze the keywords used by your competitors to identify opportunities and gaps in the market.

5. **User Intent**: Consider the search intent behind each keyword and create content that aligns with user needs and preferences.

On-Page SEO Optimization

On-page SEO refers to optimization techniques applied directly to your website's content and HTML source code. Here's how to optimize your affiliate marketing content on-page:

1. **Title Tags**: Craft compelling, keyword-rich title tags that accurately describe the content of each page.

2. **Meta Descriptions**: Write persuasive meta descriptions that entice users to click through from search engine results.

3. **Headings and Subheadings**: Use descriptive headings and subheadings (H1, H2, H3) to organize content and improve readability.

4. **URL Structure**: Create clean, descriptive URLs that include relevant keywords and make it easy for

users and search engines to understand the page's content.

5. **Image Optimization**: Optimize images by using descriptive filenames, alt tags, and captions to improve accessibility and keyword relevance.

Off-Page SEO Strategies

Off-page SEO involves optimizing factors outside of your website that influence search engine rankings. Implement the following off-page SEO strategies to boost your affiliate marketing efforts:

1. **Link Building**: Earn high-quality backlinks from authoritative websites within your niche through guest blogging, content promotion, and influencer outreach.

2. **Social Signals**: Leverage social media platforms to promote your content, attract engagement, and increase visibility.

3. **Online Reputation Management**: Monitor and manage your online reputation by responding to reviews, addressing feedback, and building trust with your audience.

4. **Local SEO**: If applicable, optimize your website for local search by claiming and optimizing your Google My Business listing and obtaining citations from local directories.

5. **Content Promotion**: Actively promote your content through email marketing, social media advertising, and other channels to increase visibility and attract traffic.

Tracking and Analyzing SEO Performance

Tracking and analyzing SEO performance is essential for measuring the effectiveness of your efforts and identifying areas for improvement. Here's how to track and analyze SEO performance for your affiliate marketing website:

1. **Set Goals**: Establish clear, measurable goals for your SEO efforts, such as increasing organic traffic, improving search engine rankings, or boosting affiliate conversions.

2. **Use Analytics Tools**: Utilize tools such as Google Analytics, Google Search Console, and

third-party SEO platforms to monitor website traffic, keyword rankings, and other relevant metrics.

3. **Track Conversions**: Set up conversion tracking to monitor affiliate link clicks, sales, and other conversion actions attributed to organic search traffic.

4. **Monitor Trends**: Stay informed about industry trends, algorithm updates, and competitor strategies to adapt your SEO tactics accordingly.

5. **Regular Reporting:** Generate regular reports to track progress towards your SEO goals, identify areas of success, and pinpoint areas for improvement.

CHAPTER SIX

Promoting Affiliate Links

Promoting affiliate links effectively is essential for maximizing revenue and achieving success in the competitive world of affiliate marketing. With this, you can expand your reach, engage your audience, and drive conversions.

Promoting affiliate links involves strategically sharing them with your audience in ways that drive clicks and conversions. Here are some effective strategies to promote your affiliate links:

1. **Contextual Integration**: Integrate affiliate links naturally within relevant content, such as blog posts, product reviews, and tutorials, to provide value to your audience and increase click-through rates.

2. **Call-to-Action (CTA)**: Incorporate clear and compelling calls-to-action that prompt users to click on your affiliate links. Try out a variety of CTAs to see which ones your audience responds to the best.

3. **Visual Content**: Utilize visually appealing content formats such as images, infographics, and videos to showcase products and services and encourage affiliate link clicks.

4. **Social Proof**: Highlight user testimonials, reviews, or success stories to build trust and credibility with your audience, increasing the likelihood of affiliate link conversions.

5. **Limited-Time Offers**: Create a sense of urgency by promoting limited-time offers, discounts, or promotions associated with your affiliate links to encourage immediate action.

Utilizing Social Media Marketing

Social media platforms offer powerful tools for promoting affiliate links, engaging with your audience, and driving traffic to your affiliate partners. Here's how to leverage social media marketing effectively:

1. **Choose the Right Platforms**: Identify social media platforms that align with your target audience and niche. Focus your efforts on platforms where your audience is most active, whether it's

Facebook, Instagram, Twitter, LinkedIn, or Pinterest.

2. **Engaging Content**: Create engaging and shareable content that resonates with your audience's interests and preferences. Use a mix of text, images, videos, and interactive content to captivate your followers.

3. **Affiliate Link Placement**: Share affiliate links strategically within your social media posts, captions, and stories. Ensure that your affiliate promotions comply with each platform's guidelines and regulations.

4. **Influencer Collaborations**: Partner with influencers or micro-influencers in your niche to reach a wider audience and amplify your affiliate promotions. Collaborate on sponsored posts, product reviews, or giveaways to leverage their credibility and influence.

5. **Community Engagement**: Foster meaningful interactions with your social media followers by responding to comments, questions, and messages promptly. Create a feeling of community around your brand to promote advocacy and adherence.

Implementing Email Marketing Campaigns

Email marketing remains one of the most effective channels for promoting affiliate links, nurturing relationships with your audience, and driving conversions. Here's how you put effective email marketing strategies into action:

1. **Build a Quality Email List**: Cultivate an engaged and segmented email list by offering valuable incentives such as lead magnets, exclusive content, or discounts in exchange for email sign-ups.

2. **Personalized Content**: Tailor your email content to the interests, preferences, and behaviors of your subscribers. Segment your email list based on demographics, purchase history, or engagement level to deliver personalized recommendations and promotions.

3. **Create attention-grabbing subject lines**: Create attention-grabbing subject lines for your emails that will persuade recipients to open them. Experiment with different subject line formulas, such as curiosity, urgency, or benefit-driven, to optimize open rates.

4. **Clear Call-to-Action**: Include clear and prominent calls-to-action in your emails that direct

subscribers to click on your affiliate links. Use persuasive language and visual cues to encourage action.

5. **Test and Iterate**: Continuously test different elements of your email campaigns, including subject lines, copy, design, and send times, to optimize performance and maximize conversions. Analyze key metrics such as open rates, click-through rates, and conversion rates to refine your strategies over time.

Leveraging Content Marketing Strategies

Content marketing is a powerful approach for promoting affiliate links, establishing authority in your niche, and attracting organic traffic. The following are some tactics for content marketing to think about:

1. **Blogging**: Create informative and engaging blog posts that address the pain points, questions, and interests of your target audience. Incorporate affiliate links naturally within your blog content, product reviews, and resource lists.

2. **SEO Optimization**: Optimize your blog posts for search engines by conducting keyword

research, optimizing meta tags, headings, and URLs, and building high-quality backlinks to improve organic visibility and traffic.

3. **Guest Blogging**: Contribute guest posts to authoritative websites and blogs within your niche to expand your reach, build backlinks, and drive referral traffic to your affiliate links.

4. **Content Upgrades**: Offer valuable content upgrades such as ebooks, checklists, or templates to incentivize email sign-ups and drive traffic to affiliate offers embedded within the content upgrades.

5. **Multimedia Content**: Diversify your content formats to include videos, podcasts, infographics, and webinars to cater to different learning preferences and attract a wider audience. Embed affiliate links within multimedia content where appropriate.

Exploring Paid Advertising Options

Paid advertising can accelerate your affiliate marketing efforts by reaching targeted audiences quickly and efficiently. Investigate the following options for paid advertising:

1. **Pay-Per-Click (PPC) Advertising**: Launch PPC campaigns on platforms such as Google Ads or Bing Ads to bid on keywords related to your affiliate offers and drive targeted traffic to your website or landing pages.

2. **Social Media Advertising**: Invest in paid advertising on social media platforms such as Facebook Ads, Instagram Ads, or LinkedIn Ads to target specific demographics, interests, or behaviors and promote your affiliate offers to relevant audiences.

3. **Display Advertising**: Run display ad campaigns on ad networks or websites within your niche to increase brand visibility, drive traffic, and attract potential customers to your affiliate links.

4. **Native Advertising**: Utilize native advertising platforms such as Taboola or Outbrain to promote your content or affiliate offers in a non-disruptive manner within editorial content or sponsored placements.

5. **Affiliate Network Advertising**: Some affiliate networks offer advertising opportunities within their platforms, allowing you to reach a targeted audience of publishers and advertisers interested in affiliate offers.

CHAPTER SEVEN

Best Practices and Strategies

Affiliate marketing has evolved into a dynamic and lucrative industry, offering opportunities for individuals and businesses to monetize their online presence. However, succeeding in affiliate marketing requires more than just promoting products and earning commissions. It demands a strategic approach, commitment to quality, transparency, and continuous adaptation to industry trends. In this guide, we'll explore the best practices and strategies for achieving success in affiliate marketing.

1. Disclosing Affiliate Relationships

Transparency is key to building trust with your audience and maintaining credibility as an affiliate marketer. Disclosing affiliate relationships ensures that your audience understands when you stand to benefit financially from promoting a product or service. Here are some best practices for disclosing affiliate relationships:

- **Clear Disclosure**: Clearly disclose your affiliate relationships in a prominent and easily understandable manner. Use language such as "This post contains affiliate links" or "As an affiliate, I may earn a commission from purchases made through the links on this page."

- **Disclosure Placement**: Place disclosure statements near affiliate links or prominently within content to ensure visibility and transparency.

- **Consistency**: Maintain consistency in disclosing affiliate relationships across all platforms and channels, including websites, social media profiles, and email communications.

- **Honesty**: Be honest and upfront about your experiences with the products or services you promote. Avoid making exaggerated claims or endorsements that mislead your audience.

2. Focusing on Quality Content:

Excellent content is the cornerstone of an effective affiliate marketing strategy. By providing valuable, informative, and engaging content, you can attract and retain a loyal audience, build authority in your niche, and drive conversions. Here are some tips for creating quality content:

- **Audience-Centric Approach**: Understand the needs, interests, and preferences of your target audience. Tailor your content to address their pain points, answer their questions, and provide solutions to their problems.

- **Originality**: Create original and unique content that sets you apart from competitors. Avoid duplicating content or simply regurgitating information found elsewhere.

- **Value Proposition**: Clearly communicate the value proposition of the products or services you promote. Highlight their benefits, features, and advantages to help your audience make informed purchasing decisions.

- **Multimedia Content**: Diversify your content formats to cater to different learning styles and preferences. Incorporate text, images, videos, infographics, and interactive elements to enhance engagement and comprehension.

- **Evergreen Content**: Invest in creating evergreen content that remains relevant and valuable to your audience over time. Evergreen content can continue to attract traffic and generate affiliate revenue long after it's published.

3. Testing and Tracking Performance

Testing and tracking performance are essential for optimizing your affiliate marketing efforts, identifying areas for improvement, and maximizing revenue. Here are some key metrics to track and strategies for testing performance:

- **Click-Through Rate (CTR)**: Monitor the CTR of your affiliate links to gauge their effectiveness in attracting clicks from your audience. Test different placement, wording, and design to optimize CTR.

- **Conversion Rate**: Track the conversion rate of your affiliate links to measure their success in driving desired actions, such as purchases or sign-ups. Experiment with different offers, CTAs, and landing pages to improve conversion rates.

- **Revenue and Earnings**: Keep a close eye on your affiliate revenue and earnings to assess the overall performance of your affiliate marketing campaigns. Analyze trends, patterns, and fluctuations to identify opportunities for growth.

- **Split Testing**: Conduct A/B tests or split tests to compare different variations of your content, CTAs, or offers and determine which performs better. Test each component separately in order to identify variables and get useful results.

- **Tracking Tools**: Utilize tracking tools such as Google Analytics, affiliate network dashboards, and third-party analytics platforms to gather data, analyze performance metrics, and make data-driven decisions.

4. Staying Updated with Industry Trends

The affiliate marketing landscape is constantly evolving, with new technologies, strategies, and regulations shaping the industry. Staying updated with industry trends is crucial for remaining competitive and adapting to changing market dynamics. Here are a few methods for keeping up with market trends:

- **Industry Publications and Blogs**: Follow industry publications, blogs, and forums dedicated to affiliate marketing to stay abreast of the latest news, insights, and best practices.

- **Networking Events and Conferences**: Attend affiliate marketing conferences, summits, and networking events to connect with industry professionals, exchange ideas, and learn from experts in the field.

- **Webinars and Workshops**: Participate in webinars, workshops, and online courses focused on affiliate marketing to acquire new skills, gain valuable insights, and stay updated on emerging trends.

- **Social Media and Online Communities**: Join social media groups, forums, and online communities dedicated to affiliate marketing to engage with peers, share experiences, and discuss industry trends.

- **Continuous Learning**: Cultivate a mindset of continuous learning and self-improvement by investing in your education and professional development. Stay curious, explore new ideas, and seek opportunities to expand your knowledge and expertise.

Lastly,
Achieving success in affiliate marketing requires a multifaceted approach that encompasses transparency, quality content, testing, tracking, and continuous learning. With this guide, you can position yourself for long-term success in the dynamic and competitive world of affiliate marketing. Stay committed to providing value to your audience, building trust, and adapting to changes in the industry, and you'll unlock the full potential of affiliate marketing as a revenue-generating channel.

CHAPTER EIGHT

Overcoming Challenges in Affiliate Marketing

Affiliate marketing is a dynamic and lucrative field, offering entrepreneurs and businesses an opportunity to earn passive income by promoting products or services. But like with every business endeavor, there are some difficulties involved. From fierce competition to rejection and regulatory hurdles, navigating the affiliate marketing landscape requires resilience, strategy, and adaptability. Let's dive into the following below;

1. **Saturation and Competition**: The affiliate marketing space is increasingly crowded, making it challenging for newcomers to stand out. To overcome saturation, focus on niche markets with less competition. Conduct thorough market research to identify underserved niches and tailor your strategies accordingly.

2. **Quality Content Creation**: Producing high-quality content that engages audiences is crucial for success in affiliate marketing. Invest time

and resources in creating valuable content that educates, entertains, or solves a problem for your audience. Utilize various formats such as blog posts, videos, podcasts, and social media to diversify your content strategy.

3. **Building Trust and Credibility**: Building trust with your audience is essential for long-term success in affiliate marketing. Provide honest reviews and recommendations, disclose your affiliate relationships transparently, and prioritize the needs and interests of your audience over profit.

Dealing with Competition

1. **Differentiate Your Brand**: Identify your unique selling proposition (USP) and leverage it to differentiate yourself from competitors. Whether it's your expertise, personalized approach, or exclusive offers, highlighting what sets you apart can help attract and retain customers.

2. **Collaborate and Network**: Forming strategic partnerships with complementary brands or fellow affiliates can help expand your reach and mitigate competition. Look for opportunities to collaborate on joint ventures, cross-promotions, or affiliate

programs to mutually benefit from each other's audience and expertise.

Handling Rejection and Setbacks

1. **Develop Resilience**: Rejection is inevitable in affiliate marketing, whether it's from declined partnership applications or low conversion rates. Instead of viewing rejection as a failure, reframe it as a learning opportunity. Analyze what went wrong, adjust your strategies accordingly, and persist in your efforts.

2. **Focus on Long-Term Goals**: Setbacks are temporary obstacles on the path to success. Stay focused on your long-term goals and maintain a positive mindset during challenging times. Celebrate small victories, stay adaptable, and remain committed to continuous improvement.

Addressing-Regulatory,and Compliance Issues

1. **Stay Informed**: Affiliate marketing is subject to various regulations and compliance standards, including FTC guidelines on disclosure and GDPR requirements for data protection. Stay informed

about relevant laws and regulations that govern your industry and ensure compliance to avoid legal repercussions.

2. **Implement Compliance Measures**: Incorporate compliance measures into your affiliate marketing practices from the outset. Clearly disclose your affiliate relationships to your audience, use GDPR-compliant data collection and processing methods, and stay updated on any changes to regulatory requirements.

CHAPTER NINE

Advanced Affiliate Marketing Techniques

Mastering advanced affiliate marketing techniques requires a comprehensive understanding of SEO, CRO, scaling strategies, and alternative revenue streams. By implementing advanced SEO strategies, optimizing conversion rates, scaling your business efficiently, and exploring diverse income streams, affiliate marketers can unlock new growth opportunities and stay ahead in an increasingly competitive landscape.

Adaptability, innovation, and strategic thinking are key to achieving long-term success and sustainability in the dynamic world of affiliate marketing. As the affiliate marketing landscape continues to evolve, mastering advanced techniques is crucial for staying ahead of the competition and maximizing revenue potential. This guide will delve into the intricacies of advanced affiliate marketing tactics.

Advanced SEO Strategies

1. **Long-Tail Keyword Targeting**: While targeting high-volume keywords is essential, incorporating long-tail keywords can enhance your SEO strategy. Long-tail keywords are more specific and typically have lower competition, allowing you to capture highly targeted traffic and improve your chances of conversion.

2. **Semantic SEO**: Search engines are increasingly prioritizing semantic search, which focuses on understanding user intent and context. Incorporate semantic SEO techniques such as natural language processing, schema markup, and entity optimization to improve your website's visibility and relevance in search results.

3. **Structured Data Markup**: Implementing structured data markup can enhance your website's appearance in search results and increase click-through rates. Utilize schema markup to provide search engines with additional context about your content, such as product reviews, ratings, and pricing information.

Exploring-Conversion-Rate Optimization (CRO)

1. **User Experience Optimization**: Improving the user experience (UX) of your website is integral to CRO. Streamline navigation, minimize load times, optimize mobile responsiveness, and create clear and compelling calls-to-action (CTAs) to guide visitors through the conversion funnel.

2. **A/B Testing**: Conducting A/B tests allows you to experiment with different variations of your website elements and measure their impact on conversion rates. Test elements such as headlines, CTAs, images, colors, and layouts to identify the most effective combinations for maximizing conversions.

3. **Personalization and Targeting**: Leverage data analytics and user segmentation to personalize the user experience and tailor content and offers based on individual preferences and behavior. Implement dynamic content, personalized recommendations, and targeted messaging to increase relevance and engagement.

Scaling Your Affiliate Marketing Business

1. **Automation and Outsourcing**: As your affiliate marketing business grows, automation and outsourcing can help streamline operations and free up time for strategic tasks. Automate repetitive processes such as email marketing, social media posting, and analytics reporting, and outsource tasks that require specialized skills or expertise.

2. **Diversification of Traffic Sources**: Relying solely on one traffic source leaves your business vulnerable to fluctuations and algorithm changes. Diversify your traffic sources by leveraging multiple channels such as organic search, paid advertising, social media, email marketing, and influencer partnerships to mitigate risk and maximize reach.

Exploring Alternative Revenue Streams

1. **Digital Products and Service**s: In addition to affiliate commissions, explore opportunities to monetize your expertise by creating and selling digital products or services. Offer online courses,

e-books, consulting services, or membership subscriptions related to your niche to generate additional revenue streams.

2. **Sponsored Content and Brand Collaborations**: Collaborate with brands on sponsored content, sponsored reviews, or brand ambassadorships to diversify your income streams and forge strategic partnerships. Ensure that sponsored content aligns with your audience's interests and maintains transparency and authenticity

CHAPTER TEN

Affiliate Marketing Tools and Resources

Affiliate marketing has become a cornerstone of many online businesses' strategies, offering opportunities for both businesses and individuals to earn revenue. To succeed in affiliate marketing, one needs the right tools, resources, and networks. In this comprehensive guide, we'll explore the essential components of affiliate marketing and provide insights into various tools and resources available.

1. Affiliate Networks and Platforms

Affiliate networks serve as intermediaries between affiliates (publishers) and merchants (advertisers). They provide a platform for affiliates to find products to promote and for merchants to reach a wider audience. Some popular affiliate networks include:

- **Amazon Associates**: One of the largest affiliate networks, Amazon Associates offers a wide range of products to promote, making it ideal for various niches.

- **ShareASale**: Known for its user-friendly interface and diverse product offerings, ShareASale connects affiliates with merchants across different industries.

- **Commission Junction (CJ)**: CJ Affiliate, formerly known as Commission Junction, is a well-established network offering a vast selection of advertisers and advanced reporting features.

- **Rakuten Advertising**: Formerly known as Rakuten Affiliate Network, this platform provides access to a global network of advertisers and offers various commission structures.

- **ClickBank**: ClickBank specializes in digital products, making it a preferred choice for affiliates in niches such as health, fitness, and self-help.

2. SEO Tools and Analytic Software

Search engine optimization (SEO) plays a crucial role in affiliate marketing success by helping affiliates attract organic traffic to their websites.

Below are some essential SEO tools and analytics software:

- **Google Analytics**: A powerful tool for tracking website traffic, user behavior, and conversion data. It offers insights into audience demographics, acquisition channels, and more.

- **SEMrush**: SEMrush provides competitive analysis, keyword research, backlink analysis, and site auditing tools to improve SEO performance.

- **Ahrefs**: A comprehensive SEO toolset offering features like keyword research, competitor analysis, rank tracking, and site auditing.

- **Moz Pro**: Moz Pro offers a suite of SEO tools, including keyword research, link building, and site optimization tools, along with insightful analytics.

- **Yoast SEO**: A popular WordPress plugin that helps optimize on-page SEO elements such as titles, meta descriptions, and content readability.

3. Content Creation and Marketing Tools

Compelling content is essential for engaging audiences and driving affiliate sales. Here are some tools to streamline content creation and marketing efforts:

- **Canva**: Canva is a user-friendly design tool that allows affiliates to create professional-looking graphics, social media posts, and promotional materials.

- **Grammarly**: Grammarly helps improve writing by detecting grammar, spelling, and punctuation errors, ensuring high-quality content.

- **Buffer**: Buffer simplifies social media scheduling and management, allowing affiliates to share content across multiple platforms and engage with their audience effectively.

- **BuzzSumo**: BuzzSumo helps identify trending topics and content ideas in a particular niche, enabling affiliates to create relevant and engaging content.

- **Hootsuite**: Hootsuite is a social media management platform that allows scheduling posts, monitoring mentions, and analyzing social media performance.

4. Education Resources and Communities

Success in affiliate marketing requires ongoing education and networking. Here are some educational resources and communities for affiliates:

- **Affiliate Marketing Forums**: Platforms like Warrior Forum, AffiliateFix, and Stack That Money provide forums where affiliates can discuss strategies, ask questions, and share insights.

- **Affiliate Marketing Blogs**: Blogs such as Affiliate Summit, Affiliate Marketing Insider, and Smart Passive Income offer valuable insights, tips, and case studies on affiliate marketing.

- **Online Courses and Training**: Platforms like Udemy, Coursera, and Skillshare offer courses on affiliate marketing, SEO, content creation, and digital marketing strategies.

- **YouTube Channels and Podcasts**: Channels like Affiliate Marketing Dude, Authority Hacker, and Smart Passive Income Podcast provide informative content and interviews with industry experts.

In addition, affiliate marketing requires a combination of strategic planning, quality content creation, and effective promotion. By leveraging the right tools, networks, and resources, affiliates can maximize their earning potential and build a sustainable online business. Continuous learning, experimentation, and adaptation are key to staying ahead in this dynamic industry.

CHAPTER ELEVEN

Case Studies and Success Stories in Affiliate Marketing

Affiliate marketing has transformed the lives of many individuals and businesses, enabling them to generate substantial revenue through strategic partnerships and innovative tactics. In this series of case studies and success stories, we'll delve into real-life examples of successful affiliate marketers, the strategies behind their success, and the valuable lessons learned.

- Real-Life Examples of Successful Affiliate Marketers

- Strategies Behind Their Success

- Lessons Learned and Key Takeaways

1. **Pat Flynn - Smart Passive Income**

Pat Flynn is a well-known figure in the affiliate marketing world, renowned for his blog and podcast, Smart Passive Income. His journey began when he was laid off from his architecture job during the 2008 recession. Determined to create a passive income stream, he started experimenting with various online business models, eventually finding success with affiliate marketing.

Strategies Behind Pat Flynn's Success

- **Transparency and Authenticity**: Pat's transparency about his earnings and the strategies he employs has earned him credibility and trust among his audience.

- **Value-Driven Content**: He focuses on providing valuable content that addresses his audience's pain points and offers actionable advice.

- **Diversification**: Pat diversifies his income streams by promoting a wide range of products and services related to entrepreneurship, online business, and personal development.

Lessons Learned and Key Takeaways from Pat Flynn's Success

- **Build Trust**: Transparency and authenticity are essential for building trust with your audience. Be honest about your experiences and share valuable insights.

- **Provide Value**: Focus on creating content that solves problems and adds value to your audience's lives. This will attract loyal followers who are more likely to trust your recommendations.

- **Diversify Your Sources of Income**: Avoid Dependent on Just One Product or Affiliate Program. Spread out your sources of income to reduce risk and increase your earning potential.

2. **Michelle Schroeder-Gardner** - Making Sense of Cents

Michelle Schroeder-Gardner is another notable success story in the world of affiliate marketing. She started her blog, Making Sense of Cents, as a personal finance journal while paying off student loan debt. Over time, the blog evolved into a profitable business, generating six-figure monthly income primarily through affiliate marketing.

Strategies-Behind-Michelle Schroeder-Gardner's Success

- **Niche Expertise**: Michelle's expertise in personal finance and frugal living resonates with her audience, allowing her to recommend relevant products and services with authority.

- **Strategic Content Creation**: She creates content that addresses her audience's specific needs and pain points, such as budgeting tips, debt repayment strategies, and investment advice.

- **Email Marketing**: Michelle leverages email marketing to nurture relationships with her audience and promote affiliate products through targeted campaigns and newsletters.

Lessons Learned and Key Takeaways from Michelle Schroeder-Gardner's Success

- **Know Your Audience**: Understand your audience's needs, interests, and challenges to create relevant content and recommend products/services that genuinely benefit them.

- **Put Quality First**: When it comes to content development, put quality before quantity. Producing high-quality, informative content will attract and retain a loyal audience.

- **Utilize Email Marketing**: Build an email list and use it to communicate with your audience regularly. Provide value through newsletters, updates, and exclusive offers to foster engagement and drive affiliate sales.

3. **John Chow - John Chow Dot Com**:

John Chow is a veteran affiliate marketer known for his blog, John Chow Dot Com, where he shares his insights into online business, entrepreneurship, and affiliate marketing. He's achieved significant success in affiliate marketing, earning a substantial income through various affiliate programs and partnerships.

Strategies Behind John Chow's Success

- **Monetization Strategies**: John employs multiple monetization strategies, including affiliate marketing, sponsored content, online courses, and digital products, to maximize his earning potential.

- **Content Syndication**: He leverages content syndication platforms and social media channels to amplify his reach and attract a wider audience to his blog and affiliate offers.

- **Networking and Partnerships**: John actively networks with other bloggers, influencers, and industry professionals, forming partnerships and collaborations to expand his reach and grow his affiliate business.

Lessons Learned and Key Takeaways from John Chow's Success:

- **Diversify Revenue Streams**: Explore multiple revenue streams beyond affiliate marketing to create a robust income portfolio and mitigate risk.

- **Harness the Power of Networking**: Build relationships with peers, influencers, and industry leaders to leverage opportunities for partnerships, collaborations, and cross-promotion.

- **Experiment and Adapt**: Stay agile and open to experimentation. Test different strategies, track performance metrics, and adapt your approach based on what works best for your audience and niche.

In conclusion, these case studies and success stories offer valuable insights into the world of affiliate marketing, highlighting the diverse paths to success and the strategies employed by top affiliate marketers. By understanding their approaches, lessons learned, and key takeaways, aspiring affiliates can gain inspiration and guidance to build their own successful affiliate businesses.

CHAPTER TWELVE

Future Trends in Affiliate Marketing

As technology continues to evolve and consumer behavior shifts, the landscape of affiliate marketing is constantly changing. The future of affiliate marketing holds immense potential for innovation, growth, and profitability. By embracing emerging technologies, adapting to changing consumer behaviors, and navigating evolving trends and challenges, affiliate marketers can position themselves for success in the dynamic and ever-expanding digital landscape.

In this comprehensive exploration, we'll delve into emerging trends, technologies, and platforms shaping the future of affiliate marketing, along with predictions, opportunities, and challenges ahead.

1. Emerging Technology and Platforms

- **Blockchain Technology**: Blockchain has the potential to revolutionize affiliate marketing by providing transparent and secure tracking of transactions, eliminating fraud and discrepancies in commission payments.

- **AI and Machine Learning**: AI-powered algorithms can analyze vast amounts of data to optimize affiliate campaigns, predict consumer behavior, and personalize marketing efforts for better results.

- **Voice Search and Smart Devices**: With the rising popularity of voice-activated smart devices like Amazon Echo and Google Home, optimizing content for voice search presents new opportunities for affiliate marketers to reach audiences in innovative ways.

- **Augmented Reality (AR) and Virtual Reality (VR)**: AR and VR technologies offer immersive experiences that can enhance product demonstrations and drive conversions in affiliate marketing, especially in industries like fashion, home decor, and travel.

2. Prediction for the Future of Affiliate Marketing

- **Increased Regulation and Compliance**: As the industry grows, there will likely be increased scrutiny and regulation around data privacy, disclosure practices, and compliance with advertising standards.

- **Focus on Micro and Nano Influencers**: Brands are shifting towards working with micro and nano influencers who have smaller but highly engaged audiences, offering more authentic and targeted promotion opportunities for affiliate marketers.

- **Rise of Subscription-Based Models**: Subscription-based affiliate programs, such as software-as-a-service (SaaS) products and membership platforms, will become more prevalent, providing affiliates with recurring revenue streams.

- **Globalization and Localization**: With the expansion of e-commerce and digital platforms, affiliate marketers will have opportunities to tap into global markets while also focusing on localized content and offerings to cater to regional preferences and trends.

3. Opportunities and Challenges Ahead

- Opportunities:

- **Diversification of Niches**: Affiliates can explore diverse niches beyond traditional categories like beauty and fitness, tapping into emerging markets such as sustainability, wellness, and digital nomad lifestyle.

- **Data-Driven Marketing**: Leveraging data analytics and consumer insights, affiliates can optimize their strategies, personalize content, and target niche audiences more effectively to drive higher conversions and earnings.

- **Partnerships with Influencers and Brands**: Collaborating with influencers and brands on sponsored content, product launches, and co-branded campaigns can open up new revenue streams and exposure opportunities for affiliates.

- Challenges

- Adapting to Algorithm Changes: Affiliates must stay updated with search engine and social media algorithm changes, which can impact organic reach and visibility, requiring adjustments to content and promotion strategies.

- **Combatting Ad Fraud**: As the industry grows, so does the risk of ad fraud, including click fraud, bot traffic, and cookie stuffing. Affiliates need robust tracking and monitoring systems to detect and prevent fraudulent activities.

- Maintaining Trust and Transparency Building and maintaining trust with audiences is paramount in affiliate marketing; Affiliates must ensure transparency in their promotional efforts, disclose affiliate relationships, and provide genuine value to their followers to foster long-term relationships and credibility.

CHAPTER THIRTEEN

CONCLUSION

Recap on the key content

Certainly! Here's a recap of key content for beginners to start with;

1. **Understanding Affiliate Marketing**
    - Affiliate marketing is a performance-based marketing approach in which affiliates recommend other businesses' goods and services in exchange for commissions.
    - Every sale, lead, or action that is brought about by an affiliate's special affiliate link earns the affiliate a commission.
    - It's important to choose a niche you're passionate about and research affiliate programs relevant to your audience.

2. **Building Your Platform**:
    - Establish a blog, website, or social media presence to serve as your platform for promoting affiliate products.
    - Produce insightful, high-quality content that speaks to the needs and preferences of your intended audience.

- Focus on building trust and credibility with your audience through transparency and authenticity.

3. Choosing Affiliate Programs
- Research and select reputable affiliate programs and networks that align with your niche and audience.
- Consider factors such as commission rates, cookie duration, product relevance, and affiliate support.

4. Creating Compelling Content
- Develop engaging content such as product reviews, tutorials, comparison articles, and how-to guides.
- Incorporate persuasive call-to-actions (CTAs) and visually appealing elements to encourage clicks and conversions.
- Prioritize quality over quantity and aim to provide value to your audience with each piece of content.

5. Promoting Affiliate Links
- Strategically place affiliate links within your content, including in blog posts, social media posts, email newsletters, and product recommendations.
- Avoid being overly promotional and focus on recommending products genuinely beneficial to your audience.

- Experiment with different promotional tactics and track performance metrics to optimize your strategies.

6. Engaging with Your Audience
   - Foster engagement with your audience through comments, social media interactions, and email communication.
   - Listen to feedback, answer questions, and address concerns to build stronger relationships and trust with your audience.

7. Monitoring and Analyzing Performance
   - Use analytics tools to track the performance of your affiliate marketing efforts, including clicks, conversions, and revenue.
   - Analyze data to identify top-performing products, content, and promotional channels, and adjust your strategies accordingly.

8. Continuous Learning and Adaptation
   - Stay informed about industry trends, changes in algorithms, and new affiliate marketing techniques.
   - Continuously learn and adapt your strategies based on insights and feedback to improve your effectiveness as an affiliate marketer.

In addition, by following the above key content and tip written on this book, beginners can start their journey in affiliate marketing with confidence and increase their chances of success in making money online. Success will come if you continue to be persistent, patient, and focused on adding value for your audience.

Final Thoughts on Affiliate Marketing

Affiliate marketing continues to be a dynamic and lucrative opportunity for individuals and businesses alike. As we've explored throughout this guide, it offers a flexible and accessible way to generate income online by promoting products or services and earning commissions on sales. From understanding the fundamentals of affiliate marketing to implementing effective strategies and staying abreast of emerging trends, there's a wealth of knowledge and resources available for both beginners and seasoned affiliates.

At its core, affiliate marketing is about building relationships—with your audience, with affiliate networks and merchants, and with fellow marketers. It's about providing value, solving problems, and meeting the needs of your audience through authentic and trustworthy recommendations. By focusing on these principles and continually refining your approach, you can create a sustainable and profitable affiliate marketing business.

However, success in affiliate marketing doesn't come overnight. It requires patience, perseverance, and a willingness to learn and adapt. It's essential to set realistic expectations, track your progress, and be open to experimenting with different strategies to find what works best for you. Whether you're a blogger, influencer, content creator, or entrepreneur, affiliate marketing offers endless possibilities for growth and revenue generation.

Discussion Questions

1. What motivated you to explore affiliate marketing, and what are your goals in this space?

   - Understanding your motivations and goals can help guide your approach and focus in affiliate marketing.

2. What niche or industry are you interested in, and how do you plan to differentiate yourself from competitors?

   - Identifying a niche that aligns with your interests and expertise can set you apart and attract a loyal audience.

3. What strategies do you plan to implement to promote affiliate products effectively and maximize your earnings?

- Discussing specific promotional tactics and channels can help you refine your strategy and identify areas for improvement.

4. How do you plan to build and nurture relationships with your audience to foster trust and credibility?
 - Building a strong rapport with your audience is crucial for long-term success in affiliate marketing. Share your ideas for engaging with your audience and providing value.

5. What challenges do you anticipate facing in your affiliate marketing journey, and how do you plan to overcome them?
 - Anticipating challenges and brainstorming solutions can help you prepare for potential obstacles and navigate them more effectively.

6. What resources and tools do you find most valuable for learning and growing in affiliate marketing?
 - Sharing recommendations for educational resources, tools, and platforms can benefit fellow affiliates and contribute to the community's collective knowledge.

7. How do you envision the future of affiliate marketing, and what trends do you believe will shape the industry?

- Reflecting on future trends and developments can help you stay ahead of the curve and position yourself for success in a rapidly evolving landscape.

8. What are your long-term aspirations and ambitions in affiliate marketing, and how do you plan to achieve them?

- Setting ambitious yet achievable goals can provide motivation and direction as you strive to build a thriving affiliate marketing business.

www.ingramcontent.com/pod-product-compliance
Lightning Source LLC
Chambersburg PA
CBHW050315230526
45471CB00005B/2192